SEAWEED

The Secret Key to Vibrant Health

First published in Great Britain in 2016 by Modern Books
An imprint of Elwin Street Limited
3 Percy Street
London W1T 1DE
www.elwinstreet.com

ISBN 978-1-906761-82- 0
6 7 8 9 10   5 4 3 2 1

Originally published under the title: *Algues: saveurs marines à cuisiner*
By Anne Brunner © 2014 by Éditions La Plage, Paris

Translator: Drew Smith

Picture Credits
Photographs by Myriam Gauthier-Moreau, except: Alamy Stock Photo: Geoffrey Morgan, 11, StockFood
GmbH, 15, Neil Setchfield, 22; Getty Images: Peter Williams, 9, Peter Barritt, 10, Rolf Hicker Photography, 40;
Shutterstock: Lisovskaya Natalia, 4, 5, Reika, 17 (bottom), Miyuki Satake, 21 (top).

Printed in China

ABOUT THE AUTHOR
Anne Brunner specializes in healthy, organic eating and family nutrition. She is author of numerous books
on organic cookery and runs the French food blog, blogbio.canalblog.com.

Natural ❧ Superfoods

SEAWEED

The Secret Key to Vibrant Health

Anne Brunner

CONTENTS

SECTION 1: DISCOVER SEAWEED

SECTION 2: FRESH SEAWEED RECIPES

SECTION 3: DRIED SEAWEED RECIPES

DISCOVER SEAWEED

Packed with nutrients but low in calories, seaweed rates as one of today's superfoods, yet this marine plant has been a staple of coastal diets for many centuries. Discover how and where it grows, learn how to distinguish between the flavours of the best-known species, and bring the unique textures and tastes of seaweed into the food you make at home.

A TRUE SUPERFOOD

Seaweed as a flavourful ingredient clearly has an ancient tradition, but recently science has demonstrated that it has amazing health properties too. While the chemical composition varies from one species to another, and changes from season to season, there are significant health benefits to be had from eating seaweed – fresh and dried.

NUTRITIONAL BENEFITS

Seaweed qualifies as one of today's 'superfoods' – that is, a low-calorie, nutrient-dense food that brings significant health benefits when eaten regularly as part of a balanced diet. It is also packed with vitamin K, iron and calcium, all of which are great for building strong bones and contributing to a healthy heart.

Seaweed has a low glycaemic index, which means it releases nutrients and energy slowly, helping you to feel fuller for longer. Seaweed is high in fibre but low in fat and calories and, composed of the same amino acids as a chicken egg, it also contains more protein than most other plants. In recent years, scientists have also come to the conclusion that some seaweed varieties contain chemicals that contribute to a healthy gut and improve digestion.

Seaweed contains a vast number of minerals that are essential to a healthy body (including sodium, phosphorus, calcium, potassium and iodine) and other micro-nutrients (such as magnesium, arsenic, copper, lithium, sulphur, iron and zinc). Many of these occur in higher quantities than you will find in other vegetables and plants.

Similarly, seaweed is rich in antioxidants, some of which are specific to the plant, such as fucoxanthin which is found in brown algae and has been seen to burn fat in some laboratory tests. Likewise phycoerythrin is typically found in red seaweed and its possible role in the prevention of certain cancers or degenerative diseases is being investigated by scientists worldwide.

Interestingly, absorbing the nutrients from seaweed does require some intestinal adaptation, so a Japanese person who has eaten seaweed frequently all his or her life will digest it better than a European who is eating seaweed for the first time.

INVISIBLE SEAWEED

It may surprise you to find that you already consume quite a lot of seaweed without actually knowing it, in the form of agar. Used in various processed foods, agar also offers an ecological, vegetarian alternative to gelatine. It has fewer calories and is helpful in slimming, because it generates a feeling a satiety thanks to its absorbent qualities.

Just one gram of seaweed contains your daily iodine needs – an otherwise hard-to-come-by nutrient.

SEAWEED AROUND THE WORLD

Seaweed has played a role in diets across the globe for thousands of years. For many coastal communities it was, and still is, a natural resource that was easily harvested and eaten fresh, or stored dried for harsher times. It may be that past cultures also recognized the health benefits that are now being considered when classing seaweed as a superfood.

ANCIENT TRADITIONS

The first records of people eating seaweed come from Asia, where fragments of fossilized laver or nori dating back 10,000 years have been found in burial mounds at Kyong-Ju in South Korea.

Eastern cultures have always placed a high value on sea vegetables. Seaweed, in particular, was a symbol of wealth, health and longevity; a gift worthy of an emperor.

Native Americans used seaweed to smother shellfish and cook it on hot stones in the ground – the original pit bake. The minerals and vitamins found in sea plants would have been important supplements to an early diet.

In excavations at Monte Verde in southern Chile, where the ruins date back to 1,000 BC, seaweed was found in the remnants of bread. Powdered forms were also discovered, so perhaps this superfood was already being used for medicinal purposes.

Traditionally, in Scotland, seaweed was harvested and hung up to dry in purpose-built, thatched huts.

People in Hawaii and Polynesia have, for centuries, eaten more than forty different varieties of seaweed and have an unrivalled repertoire of recipes to show for it. Seaweed also featured in their religious rituals.

In Europe, although a few traditional recipes exist, there is less historical evidence of seaweed consumption – except in coastal areas where the Celts knew of its benefits and thought it a blessing from the sea. Laver bread is found throughout the coastal regions of Wales, Scotland, Ireland, Brittany and France, as well as in Iceland and Denmark.

SEAWEED TODAY

Today, China, Korea and Japan remain the world's biggest consumers of seaweed, eating 5–10 g per person per day. In recent years, they have also exported the culture around the world. Only now are other countries started to take a genuine interest.

ASIAN TRENDS

Seaweed plays a significant role in daily diets throughout Asia. Kombu and nori feature the most often and are used as stock, in soups, salads and as seasonings. Nori is also a major component of sushi. Seaweed is also popular in the Philippines and Malaysia and found in many dishes.

TRENDS IN EUROPE

Ireland has a long history of seaweed cultivation and as many different names for seaweed as there are towns down the Atlantic cost. *Palmaria palmata* is also called dulse, dillisk, dilsk, red dulse, sea lettuce flakes, creathnach, or just sol. The Irish mix dulse with mashed potatoes, with fish as a chowder, and even with some cheeses. In Wales and Scotland laver bread – nori mixed

Dried seaweed has a more intense flavour than fresh seaweed and is used in smaller quantities.

with oats – was a common dish cooked for miners. In Brittany and Normandy a sweet flan was made with carrageen or Irish Moss.

THE AMERICAS

Settlers to the east coast of America brought their seaweed traditions with them. Seaweed, especially dulse and carrageen, was known as much for its health-giving properties as for its culinary virtues. In California and Hawaii, it was the Japanese who introduced sushi.

HARVESTING SEAWEED

Most of the seaweed on sale in the shops is harvested from around the Atlantic coastlines, but some of it is imported from Asia – mainly Japan, Korea and China – where the aquaculture tends to be far more advanced than in the West.

WILD SEAWEED

In most cases, seaweed sold for human consumption in the West is wild and harvested by hand. Many varieties – including those used in the recipes for this book (sea beans, sea lettuce, dulse and nori) are caught in the sea, at low tide, where seaweed fronds can be cut from live plants. This activity is largely subject to the seasonality of seaweed and the reproductive cycles of specific varieties. Kombu, which grows in deeper waters, is harvested by boat.

Fields of seaweed are not just a precious resource in their own right, they are also home to other important marine sea life. For this reason, the harvesting of wild seaweed is carefully monitored in most regions. This may vary from one place to another, but it is not unusual for strict regulations to be in force and/or for harvesting to be limited to a handful of designated sites.

Seaweed fishing boats also need to fulfil a certain number of specific criteria: each must hold a professional licence and keep records of its catch; they must trawl in areas where the water quality is sufficiently high; they must have no impact on the long -term stability of the natural habitat or on sustainability of the species being harvested.

In recent years, climate change may be a factor in apparently declining stocks of seaweed, especially of kombu.

SEAWEED FARMS

Seaweed has been farmed in Asia, notably Japan, China and Korea, for several centuries. Elsewhere in the world – Europe and the United States – this culture is more recent and generally restricted to the species most popularly used in the kitchen: wakame.

As with wild seaweed, certain regulations come into play on seaweed farms. Essentially, all practices must be sustainable, using seaweed cultures from pure stocks in order to maintain genetic diversity. Although the use of fertilizers is permitted, these are restricted to closed systems and are limited to those products that are authorized under organic farming laws.

IN THE KITCHEN

It may be that you are smitten with seaweed already, in which case this is your chance to increase your knowledge of this intriguing marine plant. Or perhaps you are completely new to the subject and wish to learn more. Either way, this compact volume offers the perfect opportunity to discover how to include this superfood in your culinary repertoire on a regular basis.

Raw or cooked, fresh, dried or fermented, seaweed is an incredibly versatile ingredient in the kitchen – its marine flavours bringing a hint of the ocean to your plate.

All kinds of seaweed are considered edible, provided they are harvested in pollution -free areas. However, while there are thousands of species to choose from, a small number are better known than others. These include nori, wakame, sea beans, sea lettuce, dulse, aonori and kombu. These also happen to be the most interesting in terms of taste.

They all feature in the recipes that follow, along with hijiki – a Japanese variety that is especially valued for its delicious flavour.

HOW TO EAT SEAWEED

While all seaweeds are suited to cooking, some (dulse, wakame and sea lettuce) are best eaten raw or in marinated form. Other seaweeds, such as kombu – which is very fleshy – and nori, are difficult to digest if eaten raw. Brown seaweeds improve in flavour when cooked. Use the recipes that follow as a guide to cooking times and methods although, in general, a few minutes in boiling water or steaming are all that's required. Note that fermented seaweeds require no cooking at all.

Served as a starter, a side, a main course or as seasoning, seaweed is not too different from many garden vegetables. It has a more pronounced flavour, however, which means it can be used in smaller quantities – a single teaspoon of dried seaweed will transform a dish in the same way that a herb does.

Brown seaweeds are particularly well known as flavour enhancers. Even in tiny quantities they are more effective than salt at bringing out the flavours in a dish.

As with all other foods, moderation and variety are key. Small quantities are usually sufficient for adding the unique flavour of seaweed to a dish, while contributing to a healthy, balanced diet.

For a guide to the types of seaweed that feature in the recipes, see our **Seaweed Taste Guide** on pages 16–21. The **Buyer's Guide** on page 72 has information on how and where to buy seaweed.

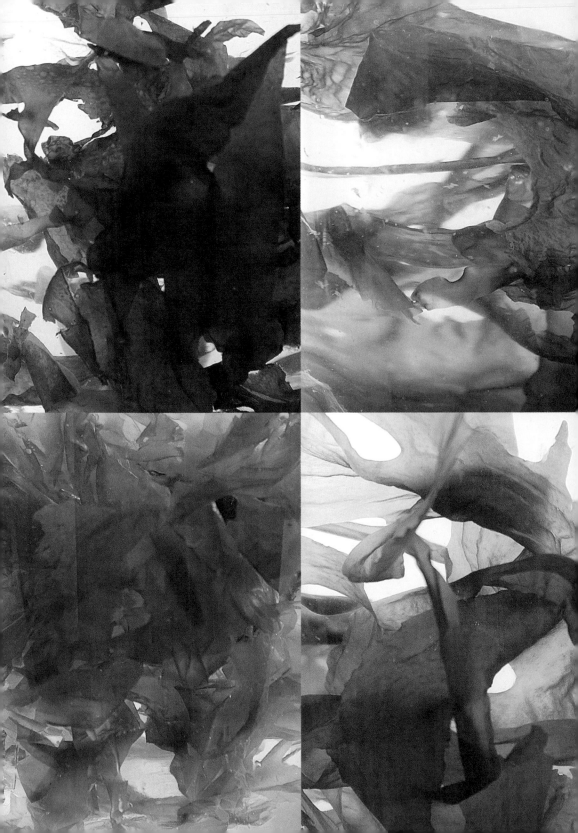

A SEAWEED TASTE GUIDE

Green, red or brown, it is not simply a question of colour on the plate. Biologically and genetically each colour is very different. You can taste the difference. Green seaweeds have a marked fresh flavour. Reds can taste liked smoked tea or mushrooms. The browns have a softer, almost sweet flavour.

THE GREENS

SEA LETTUCE

What does it look like? It is a green, blade-like leaf – thin, small and irregularly shaped, quite like a lettuce leaf.

Where does it come from? It is found around the globe. It is harvested in spring, by hand from the sea banks at low tide.

What does it taste like? It has a green flavour and is slightly peppery, it is full-bodied but only has a mild smell.

What do I do with it? Fresh and raw it works well in salads and as a crudité. Cooked in a little water for a couple of minutes you can use it to wrap other things like fish. Blended it works as a thickener and colourant in soups. Soak dried sea lettuce for a minute before using.

AONORI

What does it look like? Not to be confused with nori, aonori has long, thick threads that earn it the nickname 'hair of the sea'.

Where does it come from? Despite its Japanese name, aonori is in fact quite common around European coasts and estuaries. You can find it in shallow bays at low tide.

Where does it taste like? Mild and green.

What do I do with it? It is usually sold as a dried powder, which is easy to sprinkle on dishes or to flavour a sauce.

THE REDS

DULSE

What does it look like? Dulse is a small seaweed with a red-brown colour. Its straight leaves can grow from ten to fifty centimetres long.

Where does it come from? Dulse is widely found along European coasts down to the Mediterrenean.

What does it taste like? Raw, it has a mild iodic taste. The flavour becomes more fish-like with cooking.

What do I do with it? Cooked or raw it has many uses. Its sweetness means you can use it as a vegetable.

NORI

What does it look like? A small delicate seaweed made of a single leaf, nori can be violet to black in colour.

Where does it come from? It is native to the Atlantic and has been farmed in Korea and Japan since the seventeenth century. In Europe it is still hand-picked in the wild.

What does it taste like? It tastes like smoked tea or dried mushrooms, the more so when grilled.

What do I do with it? Nori can be used in salads although some people prefer it dried. It can be cooked in minutes and eaten as a vegetable. Its smoky flavour makes a good condiment. Dried, it can be crumbled and sprinkled over dishes.

AGAR

What does it look like? Extracted from red seaweed, agar is known for containing the gelatine-like substance used for its setting properties. Originating in Japan, it is widely used in industrialized foods.

THE BROWNS

ROYAL KOMBU

What does it look like? The largest seaweed used in cooking, it has long brown blades that reach three metres in length and thirty centimetres across.

Where does it come from? Extensively cultivated on ropes in Asia, it is also found wild around European coastlines.

What does it taste like? Asian varieties tend to be sweeter than European ones.

What do I do with it? Kombu is found fresh, preserved in salt and, in professional kitchens, is sometimes used as a wrap. It is the basis of the Japanese stock *dashi*. Thanks to its absorbent qualities, kombu's commercial applications include paper and textile making, waterproofing and as a thickening agent in ice creams and cosmetics. Soak dried kombu for around 5 minutes before using it.

BRITTANY KOMBU

What does it look like? The biggest of European seaweeds, this can grow to 3 metres in length and 30 cm across.

Where does it come from? Brittany kombu is the same species as Japanese, but is found in Europe from Scandinavia down to Spain. It grows in farms beneath the sea and is not uncovered by the tides. It is fished by boats, principally around Finistere.

What does it taste like? It has a strong iodine-like taste and is also mildly sweet. Kombu naturally contains monosodium glutamate, which works as a flavour enhancer. It passes these flavours over to food with which it is cooked.

What do I do with it? As with royal kombu, it is the basis of Japanese stock. It also speeds up the cooking times for vegetables and grains.

SEA BEANS

What do they look like? Sea beans are long narrow strips attached to a stalk that grows two to three metres in length. When harvested, they are cut down to ten-centimetre lengths like tagliatelle – earning them the nickname 'sea spaghetti'.

Where do they come from? Unknown in Japan, sea beans are found along western Atlantic coasts, usually harvested at spring low tides.

What do they taste like? They are sweet and lightly iodized.

What do I do with them? The gentle flavour of sea beans means they can be treated like vegetables. They are usually simmered in water first, for 10–20 minutes. Then they can be sautéed in a pan to colour. They also take on a nuttier flavour. Soak dried sea beans for 5–10 minutes in hot water before using.

WAKAME

What does it look like? Wakame has thin, long strands up to three metres long and up to fifty centimetres wide with indents and a thick midrib.

Where does it come from? Wakame has only recently been introduced to Europe from Asia. In Asia, wakame is usually farmed.

What does it taste like? Wakame has a delicious oyster taste, with some contrast between leaf and branch.

What do I do with it? Chopped, wakame brings a lovely flavour to seaweed caviars and soups. Soak dried wakame for 5 minutes before using.

HIJIKI

What does it look like? Hijiki resembles tiny black twigs that grow thin and short like a bush.

Where does it come from? Unknown in Europe, hijiki is imported dried from Japan, where it is gathered from the wild. Naturally bitter, it has to be treated before sale. It is typically dried in the sun, then boiled with arame (see below), which eases its bitter taste and turns it brown. It is then cut and dried again in the sun.

What does it taste like? A good seaweed for beginners, this has a soft, subtle and gentle flavour.

What do I do with it? Rehydrate for at least 15 minutes in hot water, then pan-fry or steam to make it more supple. Serve hijiki with other vegetables or in a salad, where its dark colour adds a lovely contrast. It is often served with carrot and sesame seeds as a starter.

ARAME

What does it look like? A small bush with long, flat, narrow leaves measuring about twenty centimetres long.

Where does it come from? Like hijiki, this is a wild Asian seaweed, grown mainly on the eastern coast of Japan. Harvesting is usually in summer while the leaves are still young. It is boiled for a few hours before being chopped up and dried.

What does it taste like? Arame is milder than hijiki, less iodic, gentle and elegant.

What do I do with it? First rehydrate in hot water for 5–10 minutes, and then cook for another 5–10 minutes. Arame works well in salads, with other vegetables or mixed with pasta.

FRESH SEAWEED RECIPES

Immediately after harvesting, fresh seaweed is sorted and washed – usually with seawater – to remove sand, periwinkles and other seaweed. The seaweed is then salted. This helps to remove excess water from the plant, but also softens the tougher seaweed varieties and mellows their flavour. Most fresh seaweed goes on sale in this salted state and you must remove the salt again prior to use. This is easily done by soaking the seaweed in cold water for a minute, squeezing dry and repeating the process once or twice more in clean water. Salted seaweed can be stored in the refrigerator for several weeks. Once desalted, however, it must be consumed quickly. The salads, soups and snacks that follow feature traditional recipes from the Far East, as well as a handful that have a more European twist.

SEA LETTUCE TABBOULEH

Sea lettuce is so delicate that it can feature in any salad. Here it provides a lovely seasoning to a tabbouleh for a summer lunch.

SERVES 2

200 g durum bulgar wheat

Juice of 1 lemon

1 pinch salt

50 g fresh sea lettuce, rinsed, patted dry and finely chopped

6 black olives

Cover the bulgar in boiling water and soak for 10 minutes.

Strain into a serving bowl and combine with the lemon juice and salt.

Stir in the chopped sea lettuce and the olives.

Chill in the fridge for one hour before serving.

WAKAME MISO SOUP

Fragrant and light, this Japanese-inspired soup makes the most of the silky texture and crisp freshness of wakame.

SERVES 4

1 tablespoon olive oil

4 shallots, peeled and finely sliced into rounds

1 leek, finely sliced into rounds

50 g fresh wakame, rinsed, drained and cut into strips

1 litre water or vegetable stock

1 tablespoon miso paste

200 g silken tofu, diced

Heat the olive oil in a medium pan over a medium heat and sweat the shallots and leek.

Add the wakame and water or vegetable stock to the pan and simmer for 10 minutes.

Use a ladleful of the soup to dilute the miso paste before adding it to the pan.

Add the tofu and heat through without allowing the soup to come to the boil.

GOOD TO KNOW: Miso paste is very salty, so there is no need to add salt to this soup.

SEAWEED TARTARE

SERVES 2

50 g mixed seaweed
– dulse, sea lettuce,
wakame – rinsed, dried
and cut into strips

2 shallots, peeled and
diced

1 tablespoon capers

1 gherkin

1 tablespoon rapeseed
oil

1 celery stalk, trimmed
and cut into three,
lengthways

3 endive leaves

A fresh tartare recipe that can also be served on toast or on radish slices.

Place the seaweed and shallots in a food processor.

Add the capers, the gherkin and rapeseed oil. Blend to
a paste.

Spoon the paste into the celery stalks and endive leaves.

Arrange them on a serving plate, alternating between celery
and endive as you go.

GOOD TO KNOW: Stored in a sealed container, this
tartare will keep for two to three days in the fridge.

CEVICHE OF WAKAME IN LIME AND COCONUT MILK

Wakame is renowned for tasting of oysters. This recipe really brings that out.

SERVES 3

50 g fresh wakame, rinsed, dried and cut into 1-cm strips

Juice and grated zest of 1 lime

250 ml coconut milk

1 tablespoon chopped fresh coriander, plus whole leaves to garnish

1 tablespoon chopped fresh basil

1 chilli, diced

Combine the wakame and lime juice in a bowl and marinate for at least one hour in the fridge.

In a second bowl, whisk together the coconut milk, lime zest, fresh herbs and chilli.

Pour the dressing over the wakame, mix well and chill for another hour.

Serve garnished with coriander leaves.

GOOD TO KNOW: This small, very refreshing dish works well served with rice and lentils, fried courgettes and a green salad.

STEAMED KOMBU ROLLS

MAKES 4

500 ml water

200 g sushi rice, washed and drained

1 onion, peeled and finely chopped

1 red pepper, finely chopped

1 tomato, finely chopped

90 g bean sprouts

2 sprigs fresh thyme, leaves stripped

1 pinch dried marjoram

1 teaspoon ground cumin

4 x 15 cm strips of kombu (about 75 g), washed and dried

Salt

For the sauce

75 g laver, washed

3 tablespoons olive oil

The beautiful royal kombu makes a perfect wrapper for a roll. This dish is very festive.

Salt the water and precook the rice in a medium pan for 10–12 minutes. Drain if necessary.

In a large bowl, combine the rice with the chopped onion, pepper, tomato, bean sprouts, thyme leaves, marjoram and cumin. Form the mixture into four equal-sized balls.

Place a rice ball at one end of a strip of kombu, roll up and secure with a cocktail stick. Repeat with the remaining three strips of kombu. Steam the kombu rolls for 15 minutes.

Meanwhile, prepare the sauce. Wash the laver. Cook for a minute in boiling water and drain. Blend with the olive oil. Spoon the sauce onto serving plates and top with the rolls.

GOOD TO KNOW: If you have them, you can use other sprouting beans in this recipe – mung beans work well, for example.

TOFU STEAKS WITH KOMBU

MAKES 4

500 g firm tofu, cut into four steaks

2 teaspoons mustard

2 red onions, sliced

Small jar tomato sauce (175 g)

2 kombu leaves, rinsed and dried

1 tomato

200 g farro, washed and drained

200 g rice, washed and drained

1 litre water

Salt

Preheat the oven to 180°C/Gas mark 4.

Lightly salt each tofu steak on both sides, then brush one side with a little mustard. Top with a slice of onion and a tablespoon of tomato sauce.

Cut the kombu to give you four pieces that will wrap around the steaks.

Lay the kombu-wrapped steaks in an oiled dish and arrange a slice of fresh tomato on top. Bake in the preheated oven for 25 minutes.

Place the farro and rice in a large saucepan and pour in the water. Bring to the boil then simmer over a low heat for 20 minutes.

Serve alongside the tofu steaks with the remaining the tomato sauce.

SEAWEED SALAD

SERVES 2

1 small beetroot, peeled and diced

1 green apple (Granny Smith), diced

1 turnip, diced

1 young leek or spring onion, thinly sliced

60 g fermented seaweed

1 tablespoon mustard

1 tablespoon wine vinegar

1 tablespoon olive or sunflower oil

This delicious fresh spring salad is full of surprises, with the addition of apple bringing a crunchy texture.

Place all of the cut vegetables in a serving bowl with the seaweed.

Combine the mustard, vinegar and oil to make a vinaigrette.

Pour the vinaigrette into the serving bowl and mix well to coat the salad.

GOOD TO KNOW: Lactofermentation is an old custom that uses salt and water to preserve the seaweed, allowing it to keep for weeks in the fridge.

POTATO SALAD WITH SEA BEANS

SERVES 4

250 g salad potatoes, washed

1 onion, diced

1 clove garlic, finely chopped

6 small tomatoes, quartered

10 black olives

1 tablespoon capers

100 g fermented sea beans

1 teaspoon mustard

1 tablespoon lemon juice

2 tablespoons olive oil

Sea beans are often refered to as beach asparagus, glasswort, pickleweed or samphire – and they are delicious whatever you call them.

Steam the potatoes for 15 minutes, then drain and slice.

Place the potatoes in a large serving bowl with the onion, garlic, tomatoes, olives, capers and fermented sea beans.

Combine the mustard with the lemon juice then add the oil to make the vinaigrette.

Pour the vinaigrette into the serving bowl and toss the salad before serving.

DRIED SEAWEED RECIPES

Seaweed intended for drying reaches the factory within hours of harvesting. It is first washed to remove any sand or grit and then dried at 40–80°C, depending on the variety. For sushi, nori is cooked into a paste and rolled out into thin sheets. For agar, red seaweed is dried naturally in the sun and wind for a few days before processing.

Dried seaweed keeps for several months provided it is stored in the dark and out of the damp. To rehydrate dried seaweed steep it in water or lemon juice. Smaller, thinner seaweed like nori can also be crumbled onto dishes in the same way that salt is. Agar has no flavour, but a magical power to turn any liquid to a jelly, provided you bring the liquid to the boil and let it cool to less than 40°C. The recipes that follow demonstrate the versatility of seaweed in its dried form. They include stir-fries, sushi, soufflés and desserts.

HIJIKI IN A WOK

Hijiki brings a soft, subtle flavour to this simple stir-fry, making the recipe a good option for newcomers to dried seaweed.

SERVES 2

2 tablespoons dried hijiki (about 10 g)

100 g tofu, cubed

3 tablespoons tamari

1 tablespoon olive oil

2 leeks, separated into white and green parts and sliced (white parts very thinly)

2 carrots, cut into batons

2 tablespoons sesame seeds

Rehydrate the hijiki by soaking in hot water for 15 minutes.

Marinate the tofu in the tamari for a few minutes, then drain.

Heat the oil in a wok and stir-fry the tofu. Add the leeks and carrots, then the drained hijiki. Stir-fry for about 3 minutes, keeping everything crunchy but hot.

Sprinkle with the sesame seeds before serving.

GOOD TO KNOW: Hijiki is an extremely versatile seaweed and it also maintains the majority of its nutrients (vitamin K, calcium, iron and magnesium) in its dried form.

POTATOES WITH SEA BEAN CAVIAR

SERVES 2

10 branches dried
sea beans

2 baking potatoes

Juice of 1 lemon

1 shallot, peeled and
roughly chopped

Rehydrate the sea beans by soaking in hot water for
30 minutes. They should become flexible and stand out
well from each other.

Steam the potatoes. When cool enough to handle, peel
them and cut them in half.

Drain the sea beans and liquidize with half the lemon juice,
the dulse and chopped shallot. Add more lemon juice to taste.

Dress each potato half with the sea bean caviar.

COURGETTE AND DULSE IN VINEGAR HONEY

SERVES 4

1 tablespoon olive oil

300 g courgettes, peeled
and chopped

1 or 2 cloves garlic,
chopped

1 pinch salt

1 stalk fresh tarragon,
leaves stripped

10 g dried dulse, soaked
overnight and cut into
2–3 cm strips

2 tablespoons honey

150 ml rice or cider
vinegar

Heat the olive oil in a frying pan over a high heat and fry the
courgette pieces for a few minutes to colour without softening.

Layer half the ingredients in a serving dish – courgettes
followed by garlic, salt, tarragon leaves and dulse strips.
Repeat the layers with the remaining ingredients.

Warm the honey and vinegar in a small pan over a low heat.
Pour over the serving dish and allow to cool. Refrigerate for
a few hours before serving.

CRISPY SEAWEED AND CHICKPEA FRITTERS

Here's an assortment of fried seaweed and vegetable appetizers. Chickpea flour is easy to use and makes a delicious batter. Depending on the season, you could use small florets of broccoli or cauliflower, too.

SERVES 2

15–20 g mixed dried seaweed – kombu, wakame and sea beans

150 g chickpea flour

1 teaspoon salt

1 teaspoon curry powder

250 ml olive oil

1 onion, peeled and cut into wedges

1 carrot, peeled and cut into batons

Soak the kombu and wakame for 2 minutes in cold water, then drain and cut into neat sections. Soak the sea beans for 10 minutes in hot water.

Prepare the batter by mixing the chickpea flour, salt and curry powder together. Add a little water gradually until the liquid is thick enough to coat the back of a spoon.

Bring the oil to the boil in a small saucepan. Dip the seaweed and vegetable pieces in the batter and fry in small batches. Drain on kitchen paper and serve in a tall glass.

GOOD TO KNOW: You can leave the oil to cool, then strain it and keep it covered in a jar in the fridge to use another time.

RICE NOODLES WITH PEAS AND DULSE

SERVES 2

1 handful dried dulse, coarsely chopped

Juice and grated zest of 1 lemon

125 g plain tofu, cubed

1 clove garlic, chopped

100 g peas (shelled weight)

200 g rice noodles

For homemade noodles

1 pinch salt

300 g rice flour

3 eggs at room temperature

Make your own rice noodles or buy them if you do not have a pasta machine. They are quick and easy to cook.

Combine the dulse with the lemon juice and a little of the zest. Crush the tofu using a fork and mix together with the garlic and remaining lemon zest. Leave to marinate. Steam the peas.

To make your own noodles, mix the salt into the rice flour. Make a well in the centre. Break the eggs into the well and work the dough to a smooth paste. Run the paste through a pasta machine.

Bring a large pan full of water to the boil and cook the noodles. Rice noodles cook much faster than wheat – just a couple of minutes depending on thickness.

In a pan over a high heat, quickly stir-fry the peas, tofu and dulse, and serve on top of the noodles.

GRAPEFRUIT MAKI ROLLS

MAKES 6

200 g sushi rice, washed and drained

250 ml water, salted

1 white grapefruit, halved

1 tablespoon cider or rice vinegar

1 teaspoon brown sugar

½ celery stalk with leaves

1 sheet nori

Tamari sauce, for dipping

Simmer the rice in the salted water for 20 minutes.
Turn off the heat and let the rice stand, covered.

Juice one half of the grapefruit and peel the other, removing the flesh. Mix the cider vinegar with the sugar and grapefruit juice. Heat this mixture to dissolve the sugar slightly then pour it over the rice. Mix and leave to cool.

Use a vegetable peeler to cut thin slices from the celery and keep the leaves.

Place the nori sheet on a tabletop with a large piece of paper or a straw mat underneath – this will help with the rolling. Spread the rice evenly over the nori, leaving a clear border all the way around.

Place the grapefruit sections, the celery strips and leaves at the centre of the rice and roll the nori.

Refrigerate before slicing into six sections to serve with a bowl of tamari sauce.

SUSHI ROLLING TIPS

Leave a 2-cm border clear of rice.

Spread the rice thinly and evenly.

Keep a bowl of cold water to hand. Wetting your hands and any implements will stop the rice sticking.

SESAME AND NORI PUFFS

These are great for serving with cocktails. Inspired by small Japanese crackers, they also have a certain French twist.

MAKES 6

1 packet puff pastry
(about 300 g)

2 tablespoons sesame
seeds

1 teaspoon paprika
or chilli powder

1 teaspoon salt

125 ml rice or soya milk
(or an egg yolk)

1 tablespoon soft
brown sugar

2 sheets nori

Preheat the oven to 180°C/Gas mark 4.

Unroll the puff pastry. Sprinkle one side with the sesame seeds, paprika and salt. Fold in half and roll flat using a rolling pin.

Mix the rice or soya milk with sugar and brush the top of the pastry (or use an egg yolk). Cut the pastry into strips measuring 6 x 2.5 cm. Bake for 5 minutes on a floured baking tray.

While the pastry strips are baking, cut the nori sheets in half, then cut into eight 2.5-cm strips.

Take the pastry strips out of the oven. Wrap one end of each strip with a strip of nori and secure with a drop of water. Return to the oven for another 5 minutes before serving.

BUTTERNUT RISOTTO WITH TOASTED NORI

SERVES 4

1 vegetable stock cube
or 1 teaspoon powdered
bouillon
....
1 litre water
....
1 tablespoon olive oil
....
3 onions, peeled and
finely chopped
....
300 g risotto rice
....
300 g butternut squash,
peeled and cubed
....
1 sheet nori
....
1 tablespoon crème
fraîche

In a saucepan, dilute the stock cube in the litre of water.
Bring to the boil and keep it boiling.

Heat the olive oil in a large saucepan and brown the onions
over a medium heat. Stir them well until translucent. Add the
rice and stir again, then add the butternut squash pieces.
Ladle over enough boiling stock to cover, and keep adding
more hot stock as the rice absorbs the liquid.

While the risotto is cooking, cut the nori sheet into four and
grill each piece over an open flame for a few seconds, just so
the edges curl. Set aside to cool, then crumble into pieces.

When the risotto is cooked, remove from the heat and mix
in the crème fraîche. Sprinkle with crumbled nori pieces
before serving.

VARIATION: If you prefer, replace the crème fraîche
with tofu.

GOOD TO KNOW: You can also toast nori sheets in an
ungreased frying pan – just for a minute, so that it starts
to curl and turn green.

SEAWEED PÂTÉ

This pâté is also great served on toast as an aperitif, on a blini or even with steamed potatoes. A spoonful diluted in a vinaigrette can also dress vegetable salads or pasta.

SERVES 1

1 lemon

6 tablespoons mixed dried seaweed – dulse, sea lettuce, nori

2 tablespoons water

2 tablespoons rapeseed oil

4 shallots, peeled and roughly chopped

Cut the top from the lemon. Squeeze out the juice, grate the zest from the base and reserve the shell.

Place the lemon juice, zest, seaweed, water, oil and shallots in a food processor.

Blend for a minute. Spoon the pâté into the lemon shell and chill for 30 minutes before serving.

NORI POPCORN

The nori in this recipe is subtle and simply enhances the flavours.

SERVES 1

1 tablespoon olive oil

1 handful popcorn

½ teaspoon salt

1 teaspoon nori

Heat the olive oil in a frying pan over a high heat. Throw in the popcorn and cover. Shake the pan every so often, until all the corn kernels have burst.

Take off the heat and pour the popcorn into a large bowl.

Sprinkle with the salt and nori and mix well.

AONORI RADISHES

SERVES 4

1 bunch radishes, thinly sliced

1 apple, grated

¼ green cabbage, shredded

2 teaspoons dried dill

3 tablespoons aonori

Juice of 1 lemon

Salt

As delicious as it is pretty, this dish makes a great starter for introducing seaweed to friends.

Place the radish slices, grated apple and shredded cabbage in a serving bowl.

Mix in the dill and the aonori. Pour the lemon juice over the mix.

Season with salt, mix once more and chill for 15 minutes.

DULSE BRANDADE

A classic brandade is a mixture of salt cod and olive oil, but this vegetarian option still retains the fresh taste of the sea.

SERVES 4

1 kg potatoes

250 g tinned soya or other bean

1 teaspoon thyme

1 clove garlic, chopped

1 pinch salt

3 tablespoons dulse flakes

1 dash lemon juice

250 ml boiling water

3 tablespoons olive oil

1 slice of stale organic or sourdough bread, grated

Preheat the oven to 180°C/Gas mark 4. Steam the potatoes in their skins.

Meanwhile, in a large bowl, mix the soya beans, thyme, garlic, salt, dulse flakes and lemon juice. Cover with the boiling water and leave to swell.

When the potatoes are cooked, peel and mash to a purée. Stir in the olive oil.

Drain the soya bean mix and mash into the purée.

Spoon everything into an oiled gratin dish, sprinkle with the breadcrumbs and bake for about 20 minutes.

Garnish with a sprig of thyme.

SEAWEED BREAD WITH CAPERS AND GARLIC

SERVES 6

500 g flour
....
1 teaspoon salt
....
2 tablespoons fast-action dried yeast
....
4 tablespoons olive oil
....
2 tablespoons dried seaweed
....
1 tablespoon capers
....
1 clove garlic, chopped

In a large bowl, combine the flour, salt and yeast. Make a well in the centre and add the olive oil.

Add just enough water to combine the ingredients to form a dough. Knead for 10 minutes.

Leave the dough to rest for at least an hour at room temperature or near a source of warmth (for example, a radiator in winter).

When the dough has doubled in volume, work rapidly to incorporate the seaweed, capers and chopped garlic. Spread the dough on a floured baking tray and leave to stand for another hour. Preheat the oven to 180°C/Gas mark 4.

Once ready to bake, prod the dough with your finger to make a decorative pattern. Bake for 30 minutes.

NORI SOUFFLÉ

Nori goes very well with eggs. Traditionally it is used for sushi, but also sprinkled on omelettes. This regal soufflé will convert all your friends.

MAKES 4

2 eggs, at room temperature, separated

40 g rye or other flour

1 pinch nutmeg

400 ml soya milk

80 g Comté or other hard, mature cheese, grated

4 tablespoons nori flakes

Beat the egg whites until stiff.

In a small pan over a low heat, combine the flour and nutmeg with the soya milk. Stir until smooth then take off the heat.

Beat the egg yolks and add to the milk with the grated cheese and nori flakes. Leave to cool before incorporating the egg whites. Preheat the oven to 150°C/Gas mark 2.

Oil your soufflé moulds thoroughly, including the edges, and pour in the mixture.

Bake for 30 minutes. Do not open oven door during the cooking time. Serve immediately.

VANILLA AND SAFFRON FLANS

Using agar, you can make lovely, light, mousse desserts, changing the flavours according to your whim and the seasons.

MAKES 4

½ vanilla pod, split and seeds scraped out

2 tablespoons brown cane sugar

1 pinch saffron

2 g agar

500 ml rice milk

Rinse four small pots under running water, so they are clean and will be easy to unmould.

Mix the vanilla seeds with the sugar and saffron.

Thin the agar with a little cold rice milk, then add to the sugar mix and pour in the remaining milk.

Transfer the mix to a medium saucepan, stir and bring to a simmer over a low heat.

Pour the mix into the prepared jars and leave to cool completely before refrigerating until set.

GOOD TO KNOW:

For the proper cooking of agar, mix it well with the other dry ingredients from the recipe. Mix gradually with cold liquid ingredients, taking care to avoid lumps. Boil the mixture for a few moments then simmer for a minute, before turning off the heat. The agar will turn the mix to a jelly-like mousse as it cools.

Quantities take a little trial and error, depending on how thick a mousse you like. Try 1 g to help make jam; 2 g for creamy desserts or 3 g for moulded mousses.

AUTUMN VEGETABLE TERRINE

SERVES 6

Grated zest of 1 lemon

3 tablespoons olive oil

1 teaspoon honey

1 teaspoon salt

1 pinch black pepper

½ teaspoon ground ginger

250 g squash, peeled and cut into thin strips

3 turnips, peeled and cut into thin strips

300 g kohlrabi, peeled and cut into thin strips

1 leek, peeled and cut into thin strips

1 small fennel bulb, peeled and cut into thin strips

4 g agar

For the sauce

1 tablespoon tamari

2 tablespoons olive oil

1 tablespoons flaxseed oil

Small bunch of parsley, chopped

As with many dishes using agar, it can take time for the jelly to set, so allow at least half a day to make this dish.

In a large saucepan over a medium heat, make a stock with 1 litre water by adding the lemon zest, olive oil, honey, salt, pepper and ginger.

Drop the vegetable strips into the stock and simmer gently for 10 minutes, until tender but not breaking up.

Drain the vegetables using a slotted spoon, and leaving the stock in the saucepan.

Separate the vegetables and layer them in a terrine dish, alternating the colours. Pack them down lightly as you go.

Dilute the agar in 125 ml cold water. Add this to the saucepan and bring the stock back to the boil. Continue boiling for another minute.

Pour the stock into the terrine, so that it covers the vegetables, but no higher. Allow this to cool and then refrigerate.

Make the sauce before serving. Mix the tamari, the two oils and parsley together.

Turn the terrine out onto a serving dish, slice using a carving knife and dress with the sauce.

PEAR GINGERBREAD

Cut three pear halves into thin strips.

Place the remaining pear halves, the agar and half the lemon juice in a medium saucepan. Bring to the boil and continue to boil for a minute.

Remove the pan from the heat, add the cheese and mash all the ingredients with a fork to make a purée.

Mix the remaining lemon juice with 125 ml water. Slice the gingerbread and use to line the base and sides of a cake tin. Brush each slice with the lemon water mix first.

Layer the cake with the cream cheese mix, the pear slices and the gingerbread, finishing with a layer of gingerbread.

Leave the cake to cool and refrigerate before turning out onto a serving plate.

SERVES 6

3 pears, peeled and halved

2 g agar

Juice of 1 lemon

150 g cottage or curd cheese

125 ml water

300 g gingerbread

INDEX OF RECIPES

BUYER'S GUIDE

Seaweed, especially in its dried form, can usually be sourced from Asian supermarkets and is also now available at many larger branches of stores around the UK (including Waitrose, Sainsbury's and Tesco's). Planet Organic and Whole Foods stores also stock seaweed – reliable brands to look out for include Mara Seaweed (maraseaweed.com) and Clearspring (clearspring.co.uk).

Fresh seaweed is best sourced online, unless you are lucky enough to live near the coast. There are a host of reputable online providers who will certainly be able to meet your needs. Justseaweed.com currently has the largest range of seaweed products for sale in the UK, and cornishseaweed.co.uk will supply locally and sustainably sourced seaweed.

Foraging for seaweed is not advised unless you have considerable knowledge of the area – not only for your own safety, but also for the continued preservation of the local environment.